In the Pond

Edited by Gillian Doherty
With thanks to Dr. Margaret Rostron and Dr. John Rostron
for information about pond life.

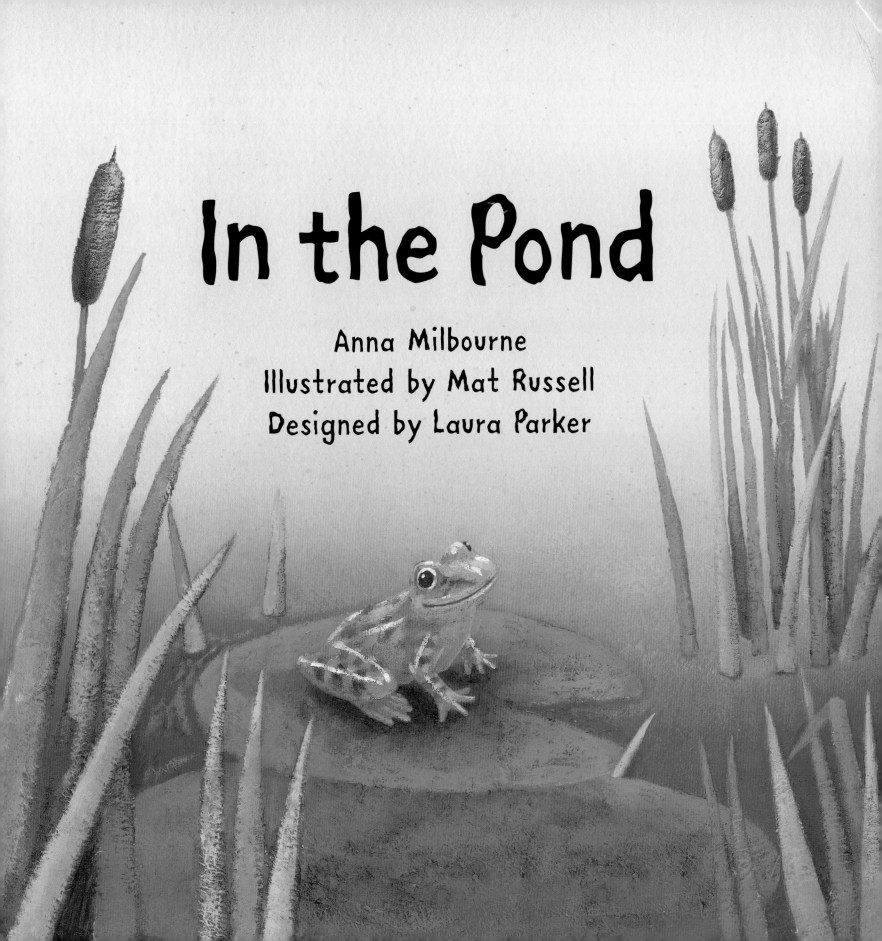

In the Pond

Anna Milbourne

Illustrated by Mat Russell

Designed by Laura Parker

Down at the pond on a bright spring day...

two swans glide gracefully along...

and ducks turn tail up,
dabbling for pondweed.

Lots of little jelly eggs
are floating in the water.

The eggs have tiny blobs inside.
What will they become?

As the days drift by,
the blobs start to grow.

They get bigger
and bigger.

Each one becomes a tadpole.

The tadpoles wriggle
out of their eggs...

and squiggle-swim away.

As the last little tadpole shivers free,
a huge, dark shadow looms above.

Suddenly, an enormous fish swishes down.

Its toothy jaws
gape open.

SNAP!

The little tadpole wriggles away just in time.

The days grow warmer still,
and spring slips into summer.

Shimmering dragonflies
dart around...

and a pondskater tiptoes
carefully across the water.

Over in the reeds there's a peep peep peep.

One by one, six fluffy ducklings
plop into the pond.

They paddle in a bobbing line
behind the mother duck.

Some stop to stare at butterflies...

then rush to catch back up.

Under the water,
the tadpole is changing.

He grows tiny legs
at the back and the front.

His wriggly tail
shrinks and shrinks.

Then, before you know it...

hops around,
exploring the sunlit pond.

A teeny-tiny fly flies by.

Quick as a flash, the hungry frog
rolls out his sticky tongue.

With a hop
and a **splash**

he dives back into the cool water.

Kicking his wide-webbed froggy feet,
he quickly swims away.

If you come back to the pond
one bright spring day...

you might find
lots more jelly eggs

and the frog, all grown up,
singing a croaky song.